This is **not** Rubbish

by **Katie Woolley** and **Sophie Crichton**

FRANKLIN WATTS
LONDON • SYDNEY

This is not rubbish.

This is not rubbish.

This is not rubbish.

This is not rubbish.

This is not rubbish.

This is not rubbish.

13

This is not rubbish.

15

This is not rubbish.

This is not rubbish.

Talk and Explore

Ask your child to describe each picture below, in their own words, pointing to each picture in turn.

Look together at how each object has been reused to make something new.

Independent Reading

This series is designed to provide an opportunity for your child to read on their own. These notes are written for you to help your child choose a book and to read it independently.

In school, your child's teacher will often be using reading books which have been banded to support the process of learning to read. Use the book band colour your child is reading in school to help you make a good choice. *This is not Rubbish* is a good choice for children reading at Pink 1a in their classroom to read independently.

The aim of independent reading is to read this book with ease, so that your child enjoys it and relates it to their own experiences.

About the book

This information book features different objects made from recycling rubbish, showing how things that might otherwise be thrown away can be reused.

Before reading

Help your child to learn how to make good choices by asking: "Why did you choose this book? Why do you think you will enjoy it?" Look at the cover together and ask: "What do you think the book will be about?" Support your child to think about what they already know about rubbish: "What do you already know about rubbish? What would you like to find out in this book?"

Remind your child that they can try to sound out the letters to make a word if they get stuck.

Decide together whether your child will read the book independently or read it aloud to you. When books are short, as at Pink 1a, your child may wish to do both!

During reading

If reading aloud, support your child if they hesitate or ask for help by telling the word. Remind your child of what they know and what they can do independently.

If reading to themselves, remind your child that they can come and ask for your help if stuck.

After reading:

Support understanding of the book by asking your child to tell you what they found out. Did they learn anything new? Did anything surprise them?

As you discuss the objects in the book, you might begin to use vocabulary such as cardboard box, plastic bottle, tube, CD, egg carton, foil, glass jar.

Give your child a chance to respond to the book: "What have you learned about how rubbish can be reused? Have you ever made something by reusing items that might otherwise be thrown away?" Use the Talk and Explore activity to encourage your child to talk about what they have learned, in their own words.

Extending learning

Have a go at making one of the items shown in the book, or another item, using materials that otherwise might be thrown away.

Your child's teacher will be encouraging accurate finger pointing at Pink 1a. Help your child use tracking to find the words that link to the information in the book. Ask them to point to each of the words in turn on each page to locate *not* and *rubbish*.

Franklin Watts
First published in Great Britain in 2021
by The Watts Publishing Group

Copyright © The Watts Publishing Group 2021

Series Editors: Jackie Hamley and Melanie Palmer
Series Advisors and Development Editors: Dr Sue Bodman and Glen Franklin
Series Designers: Peter Scoulding and Cathryn Gilbert

A CIP catalogue record for this book is
available from the British Library.

ISBN 978 1 4451 7556 0 (hbk)
ISBN 978 1 4451 7558 4 (pbk)
ISBN 978 1 4451 7557 7 (library ebook)
ISBN 978 1 4451 8226 1 (ebook)

Printed in China

Franklin Watts
An imprint of
Hachette Children's Group
Part of The Watts Publishing Group
Carmelite House
50 Victoria Embankment
London EC4Y 0DZ

An Hachette UK Company
www.hachette.co.uk

www.franklinwatts.co.uk